EMBRACE
THE PASSION
IN A
LOVER'S DREAM

EMBRACE
THE PASSION
IN A
LOVER'S DREAM

Paul Turay

atmosphere press

TABLE OF CONTENTS

EXTENDED HAND TO YOUR HEART

Winds that blow, whistle a striking tune
I dream of us hand in hand soaking the moon
Heartbeat races as I gently place my hand on your face
Reminiscing back in time, our first meeting place

A love that's deep like the sea
You are the angel that was sent for me
A blessing for a lonely soul that bleeds
I cherish your love that speaks to me

Desperation's vision, but not for long
Dares to sing a lovers song
Can your heart be where mine belongs?
Pinch me now and prove me wrong

An extended hand to your heart I send
Your love for me I pray will never end
No longer do I want to pretend
I dream to taste your lips for a final end

LIGHT IN YOU

January cloudy sky
A stranger slowly passing by
Accidentally caught your eye
Air is still and you hear my sigh

Crackling winter leaves as I slowly walk away
Your smile can brighten the coldest darkest day
Air is still as slowly I'm on my way
Winds blow as the coldness abruptly goes away

Our love story shines inside of you
Just like a star that's new
You are a dream come true
An open sky reflection of blue

Only the deepest dreams can only seem like this
An orchestrated song of love that turns into eternal bliss
The passionate strings of desire strictly on your list
We join each other hand in hand as I slowly kiss your lips

Our story now reality shines in you
A heated fire that feels brand new
Equally as one we have been renewed
I love the brightness light in you

INSIDE MY SKIN

Fall sky of September to me
Wanting to let your love in
Seems our love is so easy
Want to feel you inside in

Want to share your breath
Listen to your dreams
Hear your whispers deep in depth
Open your heart beyondthe seam

Flowers all around you
Your beauty draws me in
Fairy tale that has finally come true
Unfolding romance warmly begins

Need to share our memories
Taste passionate juices within
Story of us unlocked by loves keys
Take our chapter where we've never been

LOVE THAT SPEAKS TO YOU

Misty eyes they're froze in time wanting to get close to you
Your soul that will always shine ready for something new
Nervously waiting for a sign to move on
Let's take this step before we're gone

My heart it speaks to you
Even though you never knew
I'm drawn in and stuck on you
Standing in a fog and confused

As I wait on the sideline
All I can think is your name
Is this love or am I blind
Some will call me insane

The sands of time have thinned down
To afraid to speak or listen
I have aged for too long now
Reminiscing of your vision as it glistens

My heart it speaks to you
Even though you never knew
I'm drawn in and stuck on you
Standing in a fog and confused

GASPING FOR WORDS

She speaks to me only when I dream
The softness in her eyes, lost in emotion
Her voice it flows like a musical stream
It moves me like hypnotic waves of the ocean

I can barely speak when she is near
Heavenly body of the gods stands before me
Though I can hear her crystal clear
No words of expression performing

Gasping for words that you deserve
I am silent while you smile
Though they are written for reserve
I must somehow find my lovers style

Echoing footsteps as you walk on by
Voiceless thoughts that have no meaning
Open mouth but silence resides
As you stop and turn around focusing on the beginning

ECHOING RAIN UPON THE HORIZON

Sands they rain upon my skin
Unleash the pain that I've kept in
Afraid to speak and walk with you
Under the sun with someone new

Every day, every hour
I see your face, an overwhelming power
Magnetic rays they drag me in
Visualization is set, thought of sin

Hold hands with me, be with me
Listen to my dreams of what could be
Crawling slowly I hear you speak
I quiver and quietly you hear me weep

Misty dreams of your voice in the shadows
The echoes distanced in the gallow
I reach my hand for you to take hold
Reach for mine so this story can be told

SOFTLY I WHISPER

As a gentle breeze blows
Your smile as bright as the sun
The passion in my heart flows
I have fallen, a new love has begun

Invited by your eyes
We kiss I melt inside your skin
My love for you I can't deny
A special bond deep within

Slowly we get closer
A circle of passion rises
Don't want this feeling ever to be over
Love I dream always hypnotizes

Softly I gaze over you at night
Undertow of passion draws me in
Your breathtaking view glows in sight
Two souls that feel deep love within

BEAUTIFUL AS YOU

As lovely as the sun upon your skin
Embrace the wind that has taken in
Visions of you of internal sin
Let it flow and embrace within

Shadows fall and beckon you
Hurricane winds they flow thru
A blurry image of love of two
It blows in loves breeze of truth

Sparkle stars that brighten night
Grouped by day and decided by twilight
A chosen child but done in fright
Accept thy dues and continue night.

Kneel before the woman that completes me
Settle the score of the one to be
Echoing loudly of the one that reflects thee
Accept my hand, the troubled but lost being

WHEN YOU KNOW IT'S REAL

When you think of her before you sleep
That's when you know it's real
When your heart is hurting and her picture heals
That's when you know it's real

If she tells you she had a bad day and your heart hits the floor
That's when you know it's real
When she calls onto me craving more
That's when you know it's real

If you hear I love you without her saying those words
That's when you know it's real
If you lose sleep and can't eat
That's when you know it's real

Open heart is lost in her I think this is real
When I close my eyes and she is all I see
I believe this is real can it be?
This beautiful girl is into me

SOULS OF UNITY

Child of dawn embraced by the earth's motion
Empowering light with forces stronger than the ocean
Dig your feet deep into the beaches sand
Feel the wind blow as you reach for Mother Nature's hand

The sun has risen, slowly you feel the heat
Body of angel, so lovely and discreet
Slowly crawling until you taste each others skin
Magnetic emotion that pulls us in

Sweat that beads from your face
Our souls have been lifted to another place
Circles of fire is what we become
Flame is unity and we have become one

LOST IN ADMIRATION

It's dawn, and I awake to see your face
A distorted vision but in a comforting place
Awakened by your smile I recall
It was weeks ago, but I remember it all

It was morning on that day
Lost in your smile, I was pulled away
Time was frozen at that moment in time
Broken shell, and wishing you were mine

A bit sudden to fall, maybe it was the harvest moon
Is it too fast to admire this soon?
Words barely spoken, energy bright as the sun
Skin so fair, has admiration begun?

Trying to decipher what has transpired
This lovely woman, I am truly inspired
Dream to be the perfect man
Invisible I feel that I am

MORE THAN BEAUTIFUL

You are everything perfect, a beauty of every way
Smile of an angel that stuns me every day
A dreamers dream that lasts forever   .
Hand in hand we found the hidden treasure

LOVES SPOKEN WITHOUT SAYING A WORD

Long for the one that can not be
Blinded by her beauty light
Breathless as her eyes set on me
Her energy lights up the night

I kneel before you, time is still
You speak, words are not heard
You smile warms my broken hearts cold chill
Loves spoken without saying a word

IN YOUR EYES

Your voice echoes thru me
You're as beautiful as the summer sunset skies
Fill the emptiness my heart has learned to be
Awaken the loneliness my heart cries

Take a step closer, don't be afraid
My heart hurts like yours does too
Loves brush can't always paint loves warm, full shade
Don't turn your back on what's true

In your eyes I wish you could see me
Enter my world where a dreamer's dream
In your eyes is where happiness can be
Save me from my nightmare scream

DISTANT VIEW OF AN EVERLASTING ROSE

Breathless I am as her smile invites me
A world forgotten but have known
Want her so much as we could be
Love bottled but have not shown

Lost in your eyes I take a step slowly
Your hand slightly out of reach
Perfection you are as your petals open freely
Footprints erased by winds off the beach

Closer I crawl so I can feel you
Has fate decided the life I should have chose
Someday I wish love for me can be true
Until then I'll enjoy this view of an everlasting rose

ABOUT ATMOSPHERE PRESS

Atmosphere Press is an independent, full-service publisher for excellent books in all genres and for all audiences. Learn more about what we do at atmospherepress.com.

We encourage you to check out some of Atmosphere's latest releases, which are available at Amazon.com and via order from your local bookstore:

I Would Tell You a Secret, poetry by Hayden Dansky

Aegis of Waves, poetry by Elder Gideon

Footnotes for a New Universe, by Richard A. Jones

Streetscapes, poetry by Martin Jon Porter

Feast, poetry by Alexandra Antonopoulos

River, Run! poetry by Caitlin Jackson

Poems for the Asylum, poetry by Daniel J. Lutz

Licorice, poetry by Liz Bruno

Etching the Ghost, poetry by Cathleen Cohen

Spindrift, poetry by Laurence W. Thomas

A Glorious Poetic Rage, poetry by Elmo Shade

Numbered Like the Psalms, poetry by Catharine Phillips

Verses of Drought, poetry by Gregory Broadbent

Canine in the Promised Land, poetry by Philip J. Kowalski

PushBack, poetry by Richard L. Rose

Modern Constellations, poetry by Kendall Nichols

Whirl Away Girl, poetry by Tricia Johnson

Damaged, poetry by Crystal Wells

ABOUT THE AUTHOR

Paul Turay was born in Detroit, Michigan and later raised in St. Peter's, Missouri. It was in high school that he discovered "The Raven" by Edgar Allan Poe, and right then he fell in love with a style of poetry with deep meaning.

Paul has a lyrical and melodical poetry style that takes the reader through a profound romantic literary experience. *Embrace the Passion in a Lover's Dream* is his first published book of poems.

Made in the USA
Monee, IL
19 October 2021